SING SONG

SING-SONG

A NURSERY RHYME BOOK

CHRISTINA G. ROSETTI

WITH ONE HUNDRED AND TWENTY ILLUSTRATIONS BY
ARTHUR HUGHES

If you enjoy this book please check out our other titles, all designed to help you in your homeschool journey.

All Living Book Press titles are complete and unabridged, and presented with the original illustrations, sometimes from several sources, to bring these great books even more to life.

To see a complete list of all our releases or if you wish to leave us any feedback please visit www.livingbookpress.com

This edition published 2018
By Living Book Press

Copyright © Living Book Press, 2018

ISBN: 9781925729184

All rights reserved. No part of this publication may be reproduced, stored in a retrieval system, or transmitted in any other form or means – electronic, mechanical, photocopying, recording or otherwise, without the prior permission of the copyright owner and the publisher or as provided by Australian law.

A catalogue record for this book is available from the National Library of Australia

CONTENTS

A BABY's cradle with no baby in it	15
A city plum is not a plum	12
A diamond or a coal?	101
A frisky lamb	80
A house of cards	115
A linnet in a gilded cage	21
All the bells were ringing	107
A motherless soft lambkin	63
An emerald is as green as grass	102
Angels at the foot	1
A pin has a head, but has no hair	56
A pocket handkerchief to hem	43
A ring upon her finger	95
A rose has thorns as well as honey	121
A toadstool comes up in a night	42
A white hen sitting	86
Baby cry	6
Baby lies so fast asleep	132
Blind from my birth	91
Boats sail on the rivers	103
Bread and milk for breakfast	8
Brown and furry	41
Brownie, Brownie, let down your milk	27
Clever little Willie wee	119
Crimson curtains round my mother's bed	131
Crying, my little one, footsore and weary?	19
Currants on a bush	87

Dancing on the hill-tops	64
Dead in the cold, a song-singing thrush	10
"Ding a ding"	94
Eight o'clock	7
Ferry me across the water	96
Fly away, fly away over the sea	84
"Goodbye in fear, goodbye in sorrow"	125
Growing in the vale	20
Heartsease in my garden bed	33
Hear what the mournful linnets say	14
Hope is like a harebell trembling from its birth	17
Hop-o'-my-thumb and little Jack Horner	16
Hopping frog, hop here and be seen	58
How many seconds in a minute?	48
Hurt no living thing	105
I am a King	73
I caught a little ladybird	106
I dreamt I caught a little owl	112
I dug and dug amongst the snow	11
If all were rain and never sun	25
If a mouse could fly	75
If a pig wore a wig	44
If hope grew on a bush	70
If I were a Queen	34
If stars dropped out of heaven	124
If the moon came from heaven	127

If the sun could tell us half	126
I have a little husband	109
I have a Poll parrot	114
I have but one rose in the world	89
I know a baby, such a baby	133
In the meadow—what in the meadow?	79
I planted a hand	71
Is the moon tired? she looks so pale	123
January cold desolate	51
"Kookoorookoo! kookoorookoo!"	5
Lie a-bed	135
Love me,—I love you	2
Lullaby, oh, lullaby!	134
Margaret has a milking-pail	78
Minnie and Mattie	30
Minnie bakes oaten cakes	85
Mix a pancake	81
Motherless baby and babyless mother	130
Mother shake the cherry-tree	55
My baby has a father and a mother	3
My baby has a mottled fist	23
Oh, fair to see	118
O Lady Moon, your horns point toward the east	128
One and one are two	46
On the grassy banks	28
O sailor, come ashore	100

Our little baby fell asleep	4
O wind, where have you been	26
O wind, why do you never rest	18
Playing at bob cherry	88
Pussy has a whiskered face	68
Roses blushing red and white	93
Rosy maiden Winifred	90
Rushes in a watery place	29
Seldom "can't"	45
Sing me a song	76
Stroke a flint, and there is nothing to admire	36
Swift and sure the swallow	111
The city mouse lives in a house	60
The days are clear	39
The dear old woman in the lane	110
The dog lies in his kennel	69
The horses of the sea	99
The lily has an air	77
The lily has a smooth stalk	104
The peach tree on the southern wall	120
The peacock has a score of eyes	67
There is but one May in the year	37
There is one that has a head without an eye	74
There's snow on the fields	9
The rose that blushes rosy red	117
The rose with such a bonny blush	116
The summer nights are short	38

The wind has such a rainy sound	82
Three little children	83
Three plum buns	62
Twist me a crown of wind-flowers	40
Under the ivy bush	72
Wee wee husband	108
What are heavy? sea-sand and sorrow	35
What does the bee do?	113
What does the donkey bray about?	61
What do the stars do?	129
What is pink? a rose is pink	53
What will you give me for my pound?	50
When a mounting skylark sings	97
When fishes set umbrellas up	66
When the cows come home the milk is coming	92
Where innocent bright-eyed daisies are	59
Who has seen the wind?	98
Why did baby die	24
Wrens and robins in the hedge	22
Your brother has a falcon	13

Angels at the foot,
   And Angels at the head,
And like a curly little lamb
   My pretty babe in bed.

Love me, — I love you,
  Love me, my baby;
Sing it high, sing it low,
  Sing it as may be.

Mother's arms under you,
  Her eyes above you;
Sing it high, sing it low,
  Love me — I love you.

My baby has a father and a mother,
    Rich little baby!
Fatherless, motherless, I know another
    Forlorn as may be:
    Poor little baby!

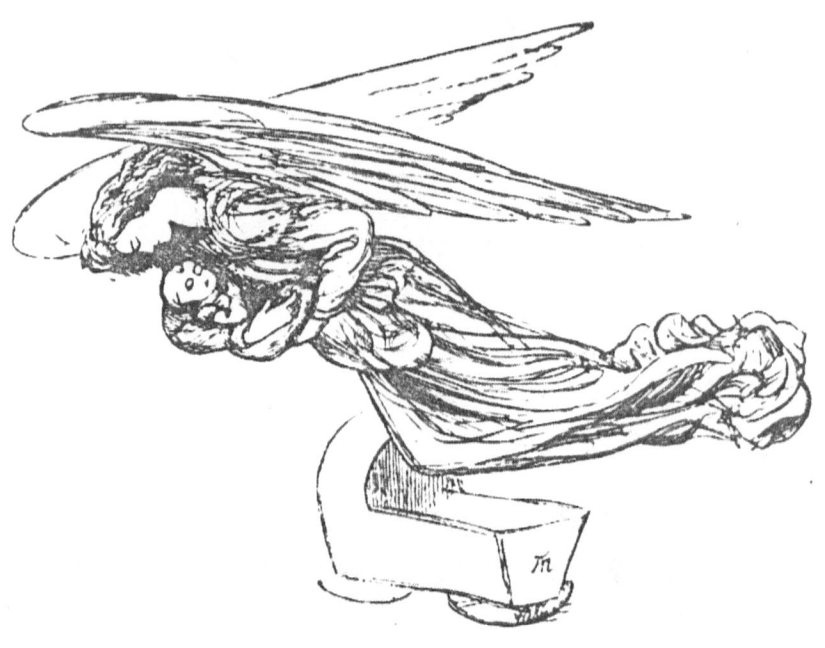

Our little baby fell asleep,
  And may not wake again
For days and days, and weeks and weeks;
  But then he'll wake again,
And come with his own pretty look,
  And kiss Mamma again.

"Kookoorookoo! kookoorookoo!"
 Crows the cock before the morn;
"Kikirikee! kikirikee!"
 Roses in the east are born.

"Kookoorookoo! kookoorookoo!"
 Early birds begin their singing;
"Kikirikee! kikirikee!"
 The day, the day, the day is springing.

Baby cry—
Oh fie!—
At the physic in the cup:
Gulp it twice
And gulp it thrice,
Baby gulp it up.

Eight o'clock;
The postman's knock!
Five letters for Papa;
  One for Lou,
  And none for you,
And three for dear Mamma.

Bread and milk for breakfast,
  And woolen frocks to wear,
  And a crumb for robin redbreast
  On the cold days of the year.

There's snow on the fields,
  And cold in the cottage,
While I sit in the chimney nook
  Supping hot pottage.

My clothes are soft and warm,
  Fold upon fold,
But I'm so sorry for the poor
  Out in the cold.

Dead in the cold, a song-singing thrush,
Dead at the foot of a snowberry bush,—
Weave him a coffin of rush,
Dig him a grave where the soft mosses grow,
Raise him a tombstone of snow.

I dug and dug amongst the snow,
And thought the flowers would never grow;
I dug and dug amongst the sand,
And still no green thing came to hand.

Melt, O snow! the warm winds blow
To thaw the flowers and melt the snow;
But all the winds from every land
Will rear no blossom from the sand.

A city plum is not a plum;
A dumb-bell is no bell, though dumb;
A party rat is not a rat;
A sailor's cat is not a cat;
A soldier's frog is not a frog;
A captain's log is not a log.

Your brother has a falcon,
  Your sister has a flower;
But what is left for mannikin,
  Born within a hour?

I'll nurse you on my knee, my knee,
  My own little son;
I'll rock you, rock you, in my arms,
  My least little one.

Hear what the mournful linnets say:
　"We built our nest compact and warm,
But cruel boys came round our way
　And took our summerhouse by storm.

"They crushed the eggs so neatly laid;
　So now we sit with drooping wing,
And watch the ruin they have made,
　Too late to build, too sad to sing."

A baby's cradle with no baby in it,
  A baby's grave where autumn leaves drop sere;
The sweet soul gathered home to Paradise,
  The body waiting here.

Hop-o'-my-thumb and little Jack Horner,
  What do you mean by tearing and fighting?
Sturdy dog Trot close round the corner,
  I never caught him growling and biting.

Hope is like a harebell trembling from its birth,
Love is like a rose the joy of all the earth;
Faith is like a lily lifted high and white,
Love is like a lovely rose the world's delight;
Harebells and sweet lilies show a thornless growth,
But the rose with all its thorns excels them both.

O wind, why do you never rest
  Wandering, whistling to and fro,
Bringing rain out of the west,

   From the dim north bringing snow?
Crying, my little one, footsore and weary?
   Fall asleep, pretty one, warm on my shoulder:
I must tramp on through the winter night dreary,
   While the snow falls on me colder and colder.

You are my one, and I have not another;
   Sleep soft, my darling, my trouble and treasure;
Sleep warm and soft in the arms of your mother,
   Dreaming of pretty things, dreaming of pleasure.

Growing in the vale
  By the uplands hilly,
Growing straight and frail,
  Lady Daffadowndilly.

In a golden crown,
And a scant green gown
  While the spring blows chilly,
Lady Daffadown,
  Sweet Daffadowndilly.

A linnet in a gilded cage,—
 A linnet on a bough,—
In frosty winter one might doubt
 Which bird is luckier now.

But let the trees burst out in leaf,
 And nests be on the bough,
Which linnet is the luckier bird,
 Oh who could doubt it now?

Wrens and robins in the hedge,
  Wrens and robins here and there;
Building, perching, pecking, fluttering,
  Everywhere!

My baby has a mottled fist,
   My baby has a neck in creases;
My baby kisses and is kissed,
   For he's the very thing for kisses.

Why did baby die,
Making Father sigh,
Mother cry?

Flowers, that bloom to die,
Make no reply
Of "why?"
But bow and die.

If all were rain and never sun,
No bow could span the hill;
If all were sun and never rain,
There'd be no rainbow still.

O wind, where have you been,
  That you blow so sweet?
Among the violets
  Which blossom at your feet.

The honeysuckle waits
  For Summer and for heat.
But violets in the chilly Spring
  Make the turf so sweet.

Brownie, Brownie, let down your milk
White as swansdown and smooth as silk,
Fresh as dew and pure as snow:
For I know where the cowslips blow,
And you shall have a cowslip wreath
No sweeter scented than your breath.

On the grassy banks
Lambkins at their pranks;
Woolly sisters, woolly brothers
  Jumping off their feet
While their woolly mothers
  Watch by them and bleat.

Rushes in a watery place,
　And reeds in a hollow;
A soaring skylark in the sky,
　A darting swallow;
And where pale blossom used to hang
　Ripe fruit to follow.

Minnie and Mattie
  And fat little May,
Out in the country,
  Spending a day.

Such a bright day,
  With the sun glowing,
And the trees half in leaf,
  And the grass growing.

Pinky white pigling
  Squeals through his snout,

Woolly white lambkin
　Frisks all about.

Cluck! cluck! the nursing hen
　Summons her folk, —
Ducklings all downy soft
　Yellow as yolk.

Cluck! cluck! the mother hen
　Summons her chickens
To peck the dainty bits
　Found in her pickings.

Minnie and Mattie
　And May carry posies,
Half of sweet violets,
　Half of primroses.

Give the sun time enough,
　Glowing and glowing,
He'll rouse the roses
　And bring them blowing.

Don't wait for roses
   Losing to-day,
O Minnie, Mattie,
   And wise little May.

Violets and primroses
   Blossom to-day
For Minnie and Mattie
   And fat little May.

Heartsease in my garden bed,
  With sweetwilliam white and red,
Honeysuckle on my wall:—
  Heartsease blossoms in my heart
When sweet William comes to call,
  But it withers when we part,
And the honey-trumpets fall.

If I were a Queen,
   What would I do?
I'd make you King,
   And I'd wait on you.

If I were a King,
   What would I do?
I'd make you Queen,
   For I'd marry you.

What are heavy? sea-sand and sorrow:
What are brief? to-day and to-morrow:
What are frail? Spring blossoms and youth:
What are deep? the ocean and truth.

Stroke a flint, and there is nothing to admire:
Strike a flint, and forthwith flash out sparks of fire.

There is but one May in the year,
  And sometimes May is wet and cold;
There is but one May in the year
  Before the year grows old.

Yet though it be the chilliest May,
  With least of sun and most of showers,
Its wind and dew, its night and day,
  Bring up the flowers.

The summer nights are short
  Where northern days are long:
For hours and hours lark after lark
  Trills out his song.

The summer days are short
  Where southern nights are long:
Yet short the night when nightingales
  Trill out their song.

The days are clear,
  Day after day,
When April's here,
  That leads to May,
And June
Must follow soon:
  Stay, June, stay! —
If only we could stop the moon
And June!

Twist me a crown of wind-flowers;
  That I may fly away
To hear the singers at their song,
  And players at their play.

Put on your crown of wind-flowers:
  But whither would you go?
Beyond the surging of the sea
  And the storms that blow.

Alas! your crown of wind-flowers
  Can never make you fly:
I twist them in a crown to-day,
  And to-night they die.

Brown and furry
Caterpillar in a hurry,
Take your walk
To the shady leaf, or stalk,
Or what not,
Which may be the chosen spot.
No toad spy you,
Hovering bird of prey pass by you;
Spin and die,
To live again a butterfly.

A toadstool comes up in a night,—
 Learn the lesson, little folk:—
An oak grows on a hundred years,
 But then it is an oak.

A pocket handkerchief to hem—
  Oh dear, oh dear, oh dear!
How many stitches it will take
  Before it's done, I fear.

Yet set a stitch and then a stitch,
  And stitch and stitch away,
Till stitch by stitch the hem is done—
  And after work is play!

If a pig wore a wig,
  What could we say?
Treat him as a gentleman,
  And say "Good day."

If his tail chanced to fail,
  What could we do? —
Send him to the tailoress
  To get one new.

Seldom "can't,"
　Seldom "don't";
Never "shan't,"
　Never "won't."

1 and 1 are 2—
That's for me and you.

2 and 2 are 4—
That's a couple more.

3 and 3 are 6
Barley-sugar sticks.

4 and 4 are 8
Tumblers at the gate.

5 and 5 are 10
Bluff seafaring men.

6 and 6 are 12
Garden lads who delve.

7 and 7 are 14
Young men bent on sporting.

8 and 8 are 16
Pills the doctor's mixing.

9 and 9 are 18
Passengers kept waiting.

10 and 10 are 20
Roses—pleasant plenty!

11 and 11 are 22
Sums for brother George to do.

12 and 12 are 24
Pretty pictures, and no more.

How many seconds in a minute?
Sixty, and no more in it.

How many minutes in an hour?
Sixty for sun and shower.

How many hours in a day?
Twenty-four for work and play.

How many days in a week?
Seven both to hear and speak.

How many weeks in a month?
Four, as the swift moon runn'th.

How many months in a year?
Twelve the almanack makes clear.

How many years in an age?
One hundred says the sage.

How many ages in time?
No one knows the rhyme.

What will you give me for my pound?
Full twenty shillings round.
What will you give me for my shilling?
Twelve pence to give I'm willing.
What will you give me for my penny?
Four farthings, just so many.

January cold desolate;
February all dripping wet;
March wind ranges;
April changes;
Birds sing in tune
  To flowers of May,
And sunny June
  Brings longest day;
In scorched July
The storm-clouds fly
Lightning-torn;
August bears corn,
September fruit;

In rough October
Earth must disrobe her;
Stars fall and shoot
In keen November;
And night is long
And cold is strong
In bleak December.

What is pink? a rose is pink
By the fountain's brink.
What is red? a poppy's red
In its barley bed.
What is blue? the sky is blue
Where the clouds float thro'.
What is white? a swan is white
Sailing in the light.
What is yellow? pears are yellow,
Rich and ripe and mellow.

What is green? the grass is green,
With small flowers between.
What is violet? clouds are violet
In the summer twilight.
What is orange? why, an orange,
Just an orange!

Mother shake the cherry-tree,
  Susan catch a cherry;
Oh how funny that will be,
  Let's be merry!

One for brother, one for sister,
  Two for mother more,
Six for father, hot and tired,
  Knocking at the door.

A pin has a head, but has no hair;
A clock has a face, but no mouth there;
Needles have eyes, but they cannot see;
A fly has a trunk without lock or key;
A timepiece may lose, but cannot win;
A corn-field dimples without a chin;
A hill has no leg, but has a foot;
A wine-glass a stem, but not a root;

A watch has hands, but no thumb or finger;
A boot has a tongue, but is no singer;
Rivers run, though they have no feet;
A saw has teeth, but it does not eat;
Ash-trees have keys, yet never a lock;
And baby crows, without being a cock.

Hopping frog, hop here and be seen,
  I'll not pelt you with stick or stone:
Your cap is laced and your coat is green;
  Good bye, we'll let each other alone.

Plodding toad, plod here and be looked at,
You the finger of scorn is crooked at:
But though you're lumpish, you're harmless too;
You won't hurt me, and I won't hurt you.

Where innocent bright-eyed daisies are,
  With blades of grass between,
Each daisy stands up like a star
  Out of a sky of green.

The city mouse lives in a house;—
   The garden mouse lives in a bower,
He's friendly with the frogs and toads,
   And sees the pretty plants in flower.

The city mouse eats bread and cheese;—
   The garden mouse eats what he can;
We will not grudge him seeds and stalks,
   Poor little timid furry man.

What does the donkey bray about?
What does the pig grunt through his snout?
What does the goose mean by a hiss?
Oh, Nurse, if you can tell me this,
I'll give you such a kiss.

The cockatoo calls "cockatoo,"
The magpie chatters "how d'ye do?"
The jackdaw bids me "go away,"
Cuckoo cries "cuckoo" half the day:
What do the others say?

Three plum buns
  To eat here at the stile
In the clover meadow,
  For we have walked a mile.

One for you, and one for me,
  And one left over:
Give it to the boy who shouts
  To scare sheep from the clover.

A motherless soft lambkin
  Along upon a hill;
No mother's fleece to shelter him
  And wrap him from the cold:—
I'll run to him and comfort him,
  I'll fetch him, that I will;
I'll care for him and feed him
  Until he's strong and bold.

Dancing on the hill-tops,
  Singing in the valleys,
Laughing with the echoes,
  Merry little Alice.

Playing games with lambkins
  In the flowering valleys,
Gathering pretty posies,
  Helpful little Alice.

If her father's cottage
  Turned into a palace,
And he owned the hill-tops
  And the flowering valleys,
She'd be none the happier,
  Happy little Alice.

When fishes set umbrellas up
 If the rain-drops run,
Lizards will want their parasols
 To shade them from the sun.

The peacock has a score of eyes,
  With which he cannot see;
The cod-fish has a silent sound,
  However that may be;

No dandelions tell the time,
  Although they turn to clocks;
Cat's-cradle does not hold the cat,
  Nor foxglove fit the fox.

Pussy has a whiskered face,
Kitty has such pretty ways;
Doggie scampers when I call,
And has a heart to love us all.

The dog lies in his kennel,
  And Puss purrs on the rug,
And baby perches on my knee
  For me to love and hug.

Pat the dog and stroke the cat,
  Each in its degree;
And cuddle and kiss my baby,
  And baby kiss me.

If hope grew on a bush,
   And joy grew on a tree,
What a nosegay for the plucking
   There would be!

But oh! in windy autumn,
   When frail flowers wither,
What should we do for hope and joy,
   Fading together?

I planted a hand
  And there came up a palm,
I planted a heart
  And there came up balm.

Then I planted a wish,
  But there sprang a thorn,
While heaven frowned with thunder
  And earth sighed forlorn.

Under the ivy bush
  One sits sighing,
And under the willow tree
  One sits crying:—

Under the ivy bush
  Cease from your sighing,
But under the willow-tree
  Lie down a-dying.

I am a King,
  Or an Emperor rather,
I wear crown-imperial
  And prince's-feather;
Golden-rod is the sceptre
  I wield and wag,
And a broad purple flag-flower
  Waves for my flag.

Elder the pithy
  With old-man and sage,
These are my councillors
  Green in old age;
Lord-and-ladies in silence
  Stand round me and wait,
While gay ragged-robin
  Makes bows at my gate.

There is one that has a head without an eye,
  And there's one that has an eye without a head:
You may find the answer if you try;
   And when all is said,
   Half the answer hangs upon a thread!

If a mouse could fly,
  Or if a crow could swim,
Or if a sprat could walk and talk,
  I'd like to be like him.

If a mouse could fly,
  He might fly away;
Or if a crow could swim,
  It might turn him grey;
Or if a sprat could walk and talk,
What would he find to say?

Sing me a song—
  What shall I sing? —
Three merry sisters
  Dancing in a ring,
Light and fleet upon their feet
  As birds upon the wing.

Tell me a tale—
  What shall I tell?
Two mournful sisters,
  And a tolling knell,
Tolling ding and tolling dong,
  Ding dong bell.

The lily has an air,
  And the snowdrop a grace,
And the sweetpea a way,
  And the heartsease a face, —
Yet there's nothing like the rose
  When she blows.

Margaret has a milking-pail,
  And she rises early;
Thomas has a threshing-flail,
  And he's up betimes.
Sometimes crossing through the grass
  Where the dew lies pearly,
They say "Good morrow" as they pass
  By the leafy limes.

In the meadow — what in the meadow?
Bluebells, buttercups, meadowsweet,
And fairy rings for the children's feet
  In the meadow.

In the garden — what in the garden?
Jacob's-ladder and Solomon's-seal,
And Love-lies-bleeding beside All-heal
  In the garden.

A frisky lamb
And a frisky child
Playing their pranks
  In a cowslip meadow:
The sky all blue
And the air all mild
And the fields all sun
  And the lanes half shadow.

Mix a pancake,
Stir a pancake,
  Pop it in the pan;
Fry the pancake,
Toss the pancake, —
  Catch it if you can.

The wind has such a rainy sound
  Moaning through the town,
The sea has such a windy sound, —
  Will the ships go down?

The apples in the orchard
  Tumble from their tree. —
Oh will the ships go down, go down,
  In the windy sea?

Three little children
  On the wide wide earth,
Motherless children—
  Cared for from their birth
  By tender angels.

Three little children
  On the wide wide sea,
Motherless children—
  Safe as safe can be
  With guardian angels.

Fly away, fly away over the sea,
  Sun-loving swallow, for summer is done;
Come again, come again, come back to me,
  Bringing the summer and bringing the sun.

Minnie bakes oaten cakes,
  Minnie brews ale,
All because her Johnny's coming
  Home from sea.
And she glows like a rose
  Who was so pale,
And "Are you sure the church clock goes?"
  Says she.

A white hen sitting
  On white eggs three:
Next, three speckled chickens
  As plump as plump can be.

An owl, and a hawk,
  And a bat come to see:
But chicks beneath their mother's wing
  Squat safe as safe can be.

Currants on a bush,
  And figs upon a stem,
And cherries on a bending bough,
  And Ned to gather them.

Playing at bob cherry
  Tom and Nell and Hugh:
Cherry bob! cherry bob!
  There's a bob for you.

Tom bobs a cherry
  For gaping snapping Hugh,
While curly-pated Nelly
  Snaps at it too.

Look, look, look—
  Oh what a sight to see!
The wind is playing cherry bob
  With the cherry tree.

I have but one rose in the world,
   And my one rose stands a-drooping:
Oh, when my single rose is dead
   There'll be but thorns for stooping.

Rosy maiden Winifred,
With a milkpail on her head,
Tripping through the corn,
  While the dew lies on the wheat
  In the sunny morn.
Scarlet shepherd's-weatherglass
  Spreads wide open at her feet
    As they pass;
Cornflowers give their almond smell
  While she brushes by,
    And a lark sings from the sky
    "All is well."

Blind from my birth,
Where flowers are springing
I sit on earth
All dark.
Hark! hark!
A lark is singing.
His notes are all for me,
For me his mirth :—
Till some day I shall see
Beautiful flowers
And birds in bowers
Where all Joy Bells are ringing.

When the cows come home the milk is coming,
Honey's made while the bees are humming;
Duck and drake on the rushy lake,
And the deer live safe in the breezy brake;
And timid, funny, brisk little bunny,
Winks his nose and sits all sunny.

Roses blushing red and white,
  For delight;
Honeysuckle wreaths above,
  For love;
Dim sweet-scented heliotrope,
  For hope;
Shining lilies tall and straight,
  For royal state;
Dusky pansies, let them be
  For memory;
With violets of fragrant breath,
  For death.

"Ding a ding,"
The sweet bells sing,
And say:
"Come, all be gay"
For a wedding day.

"Dong a dong,"
The bells sigh long,
And call:
"Weep one, weep all"
For a funeral.

A ring upon her finger,
  Walks the bride,
With the bridegroom tall and handsome
  At her side.

A veil upon her forehead
  Walks the bride,
With the bridegroom proud and merry
  At her side.

Fling flowers beneath the footsteps
  Of the bride;
Fling flowers before the bridegroom
  At her side.

"Ferry me across the water,
  Do, boatman, do."
"If you've a penny in your purse
  I'll ferry you."

"I have a penny in my purse,
  And my eyes are blue;
So ferry me across the water,
  Do, boatman, do."

"Step into my ferry-boat,
  Be they black or blue,
And for the penny in your purse
  I'll ferry you."

When a mounting skylark sings
  In the sunlit summer morn,
I know that heaven is up on high,
  And on earth are fields of corn.

But when a nightingale sings
  In the moonlit summer even,
I know not if earth is merely earth,
  Only that heaven is heaven.

Who has seen the wind?
  Neither I nor you:
But when the leaves hang trembling
  The wind is passing thro'.

Who has seen the wind?
  Neither you nor I:
But when the trees bow down their heads
  The wind is passing by.

The horses of the sea
  Rear a foaming crest,
But the horses of the land
  Serve us the best.

The horses of the land
  Munch corn and clover,
While the foaming sea-horses
  Toss and turn over.

O sailor, come ashore,
  What have you brought for me?
Red coral, white coral,
  Coral from the sea.

I did not dig it from the ground,
  Nor pluck it from a tree;
Feeble insects made it
  In the stormy sea.

A diamond or a coal?
  A diamond, if you please:
Who cares about a clumsy coal
  Beneath the summer trees?

A diamond or a coal?
  A coal, sir, if you please:
One comes to care about the coal
  What time the waters freeze.

An emerald is as green as grass;
  A ruby red as blood;
A sapphire shines as blue as heaven;
  A flint lies in the mud.

A diamond is a brilliant stone,
  To catch the world's desire;
An opal holds a fiery spark;
  But a flint holds fire.

Boats sail on the rivers,
  And ships sail on the seas;
But clouds that sail across the sky
  Are prettier far than these.

There are bridges on the rivers,
  As pretty as you please;
But the bow that bridges heaven,
  And overtops the trees,
And builds a road from earth to sky,
  Is prettier far than these.

The lily has a smooth stalk,
  Will never hurt your hand;
But the rose upon her briar
  Is lady of the land.

There's sweetness in an apple tree,
  And profit in the corn;
But lady of all beauty
  Is a rose upon a thorn.

When with moss and honey
  She tips her bending briar,
And half unfolds her glowing heart,
  She sets the world on fire.

Hurt no living thing:
  Ladybird, nor butterfly,
Nor moth with dusty wing,
  Nor cricket chirping cheerily,
Nor grasshopper so light of leap,
  Nor dancing gnat, nor beetle fat,
Nor harmless worms that creep.

I caught a little ladybird
  That flies far away;
I caught a little lady wife
  That is both staid and gay.

Come back, my scarlet ladybird,
  Back from far away;
I weary of my dolly wife,
  My wife that cannot play.

She's such a senseless wooden thing
  She stares the livelong day;
Her wig of gold is stiff and cold
  And cannot change to grey.

All the bells were ringing
And all the birds were singing,
When Molly sat down crying
  For her broken doll:
  O you silly Moll!
Sobbing and sighing
  For a broken doll,
When all the bells are ringing
And all the birds are singing.

Wee wee husband,
  Give me some money,
I have no comfits,
  And I have no honey.

Wee wee wifie,
  I have no money,
Milk, nor meat, nor bread to eat,
  Comfits, nor honey.

I have a little husband
  And he is gone to sea,
The winds that whistle round his ship
  Fly home to me.

The winds that sigh about me
  Return again to him;
So I would fly, if only I
  Were light of limb.

The dear old woman in the lane
  Is sick and sore with pains and aches,
We'll go to her this afternoon,
  And take her tea and eggs and cakes.

We'll stop to make the kettle boil,
  And brew some tea, and set the tray,
And poach an egg, and toast a cake,
  And wheel her chair round, if we may.

Swift and sure the swallow,
  Slow and sure the snail:
Slow and sure may miss his way,
  Swift and sure may fail.

"I dreamt I caught a little owl
  And the bird was blue—"

"But you may hunt for ever
  And not find such a one."

"I dreamt I set a sunflower,
  And red as blood it grew—"

"But such a sunflower never
  Bloomed beneath the sun."

What does the bee do?
  Bring home honey.
And what does Father do?
  Bring home money.
And what does Mother do?
  Lay out the money.
And what does baby do?
  Eat up the honey.

I have a Poll parrot,
   And Poll is my doll,
And my nurse is Polly,
   And my sister Poll.

"Polly!" cried Polly,
"Don't tear Polly dolly"—
   While soft-hearted Poll
   Trembled for the doll.

A house of cards
 Is neat and small:
Shake the table,
 It must fall.

Find the Court cards
 One by one;
Raise it, roof it,—
 Now it's done:—
Shake the table!
 That's the fun.

The rose with such a bonny blush,
  What has the rose to blush about?
If it's the sun that makes her flush,
  What's in the sun to flush about?

The rose that blushes rosy red,
  She must hang her head;
The lily that blows spotless white,
  She may stand upright.

Oh, fair to see
Blossom-laden cherry tree,
  Arrayed in sunny white;
  An April day's delight,
Oh, fair to see!

Oh, fair to see
Fruit-laden cherry tree,
  With balls of shining red
  Decking a leafy head,
Oh, fair to see!

Clever little Willie wee,
  Bright-eyed, blue-eyed little fellow;
Merry little Margery
  With her hair all yellow.

Little Willie in his heart
  Is a sailor on the sea,
And he often cons a chart
  With sister Margery.

The peach tree on the southern wall
  Has basked so long beneath the sun,
Her score of peaches great and small
  Bloom rosy, every one.

A peach for brothers, one for each,
  A peach for you and a peach for me;
But the biggest, rosiest, downiest peach
  For Grandmamma with her tea.

A rose has thorns as well as honey,
I'll not have her for love or money;
An iris grows so straight and fine,
That she shall be no friend of mine;
Snowdrops like the snow would chill me;
Nightshade would caress and kill me;
Crocus like a spear would fright me;
Dragon's-mouth might bark or bite me;
Convolvulus but blooms to die;

A wind-flower suggests a sigh;
Love-lies-bleeding makes me sad;
And poppy-juice would drive me mad:—
But give me holly, bold and jolly,
Honest, prickly, shining holly;
Pluck me holly leaf and berry
For the day when I make merry.

Is the moon tired? she looks so pale
Within her misty veil:
She scales the sky from east to west,
And takes no rest.

Before the coming of the night
The moon shows papery white;
Before the dawning of the day
She fades away.

If stars dropped out of heaven,
  And if flowers took their place,
The sky would still look very fair,
  And fair earth's face.

Winged angels might fly down to us
  To pluck the stars,
Be we could only long for flowers
  Beyond the cloudy bars.

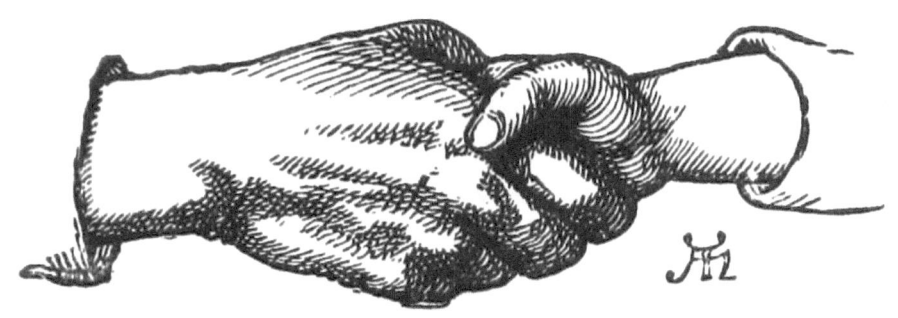

"Goodbye in fear, goodbye in sorrow,
  Goodbye, and all in vain,
Never to meet again, my dear—"
  "Never to part again."
"Goodbye to-day, goodbye to-morrow,
  Goodbye till earth shall wane,
Never to meet again, my dear—"
  "Never to part again."

If the sun could tell us half
  That he hears and sees,
Sometimes he would make us laugh,
  Sometimes make us cry:
Think of all the birds that make
  Homes among the trees;
Think of cruel boys who take
  Birds that cannot fly.

If the moon came from heaven,
  Talking all the way,
What could she have to tell us,
  And what could she say?

"I've seen a hundred pretty things,
  And seen a hundred gay;
But only think: I peep by night
  And do not peep by day!"

O Lady Moon, your horns point toward the east:
    Shine, be increased;
O Lady Moon, your horns point toward the west:
    Wane, be at rest.

What do the stars do
  Up in the sky,
Higher than the wind can blow,
  Or the clouds can fly?

Each star in its own glory
  Circles, circles still;
As it was lit to shine and set,
  And do its Maker's will.

Motherless baby and babyless mother,
Bring them together to love one another.

Crimson curtains round my mother's bed,
  Silken soft as may be;
Cool white curtains round about my bed,
  For I am but a baby.

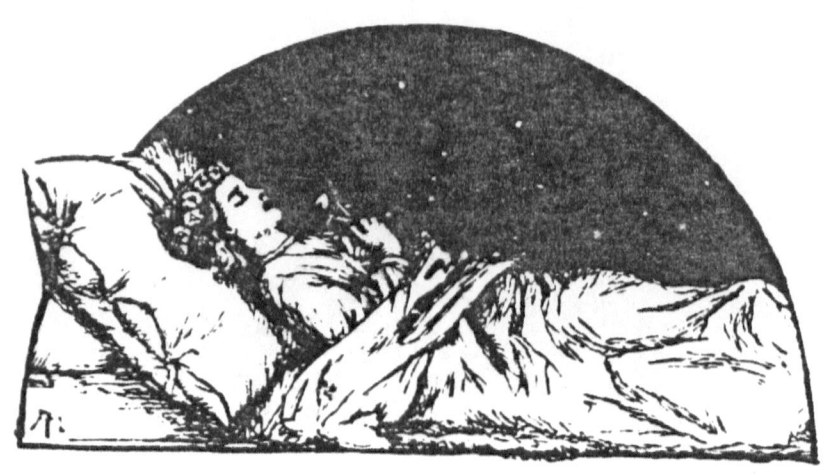

Baby lies so fast asleep
  That we cannot wake her:
Will the angels clad in white
  Fly from heaven to take her?

Baby lies so fast asleep
  That no pain can grieve her;
Put a snowdrop in her hand,
  Kiss her once and leave her.

I know a baby, such a baby,—
  Round blue eyes abd cheeks of pink,
Such an elbow furrowed with dimples,
  Such a wrist where creases sink.

"Cuddle and love me, cuddle and love me,"
  Crows the mouth of coral pink:
Oh, the bald head, and, oh, the sweet lips,
  And, oh, the sleepy eyes that wink!

Lullaby, oh, lullaby!
Flowers are closed and lambs are sleeping;
Lullaby, oh, lullaby!
Stars are up, the moon is peeping;
Lullaby, oh, lullaby!
While the birds are silence keeping,
   (Lullaby, oh, lullaby!)
Sleep, my baby, fall a-sleeping,
   Lullaby, oh, lullaby!

Lie a-bed,
Sleepy head,
Shut up eyes, bo-peep;
Till daybreak
Never wake:—
Baby, sleep.

www.ingramcontent.com/pod-product-compliance
Lightning Source LLC
Chambersburg PA
CBHW031118080526
44587CB00011B/1021